Amazing Animals

TIGERS

Sally Morgan

FRANKLIN WATTS
LONDON•SYDNEY

An Appleseed Editions book

First published in 2010 by Franklin Watts

Franklin Watts
338 Euston Road, London NW1 3BH

Franklin Watts Australia
Level 17/207 Kent St, Sydney, NSW 2000

Appleseed Editions Ltd
Well House, Friars Hill, Guestling, East Sussex TN35 4ET

Created by Q2AMedia
Editor: Katie Dicker
Art Director: Harleen Mehta
Designers: Shruti Aggarwal, Tarang Saggar
Picture Researcher: Sujatha Menon

ISBN 978 1 4451 0006 7

Dewey classification: 599.7'56

All words in **bold** can be found in the Glossary on pages 30–31.

Website information is correct at the time of going to press. However, the publishers cannot
accept liability for any information or links found on third-party websites.

A CIP catalogue for this book is available from the British Library.

Picture credits
t=top b=bottom c=centre l=left r=right
Cover images: Ludmila Yilmaz/Shutterstock,Roman Kobzarev/Istockphoto

Andrea Poole/Istockphoto: Title page, Artur Tiutenko/Shutterstock: Contents page, John Hyde/Photolibrary: 4, Estima/Fotolia: 5t,
Shutterstock: 5b, Andy Rouse/NHPA: 6, Pillai Balan/Istockphoto: 7t, Photolibrary: 7b, Satyendra Tiwari/Ecoscene: 8,
Andrea Poole/Istockphoto: 9, Pradeep Kumar Saxena/Istockphoto: 10, Max Earey/Shutterstock: 11t, Ken Brown/Istockphoto: 11b,
Stefan Ekernas/Istockphoto: 12, Mike Dabell/Istockphoto: 13t, Brian Opyd/Istockphoto: 13b, Andy Rouse/NHPA: 14,
Mahipal Singh/Photolibrary: 15, Sigge/Dreamstime: 16, Megan Lorenz/Istockphoto: 17, Steve Geer/Istockphoto: 18,
Chris Sargent/Shutterstock: 19t, Phillip Cola/Ecoscene: 19b, Ludmia Yimaz/Shutterstock: 20, Kane/Shutterstock: 21t,
Ludmila Yilmaz/Shutterstock: 21b, Photolibrary: 22, Dale Robert Franz/Photolibrary: 23, John Moore/AP Photos: 24,
Parth Sanyal/Reuters: 25t, Jayanta Shaw/Reuters: 25b, Satyendra Tiwari/Ecoscene: 26, Karl Ammann/Ecoscene: 27,
Michael Steden/Istockphoto: 28, Nick Biemans/Istockphoto: 29, Steve Geer/Istockphoto: 31.

Printed in China

Franklin Watts is a division of Hachette Children's Books,
an Hachette Livre UK company.
www.hachettelivre.co.uk

Contents

King of the cats

Tigers are the largest cats on Earth. Their orange fur and dark stripes make them easy to recognise. These powerful hunters have large, sharp teeth and claws. It is no surprise that they are called the king of the cats.

Types of tiger

Tigers are **mammals**, a type of animal that is covered in hair. The females feed their young with milk. Their closest relatives are the lion, leopard and cheetah. There is only one type, or **species**, of tiger. But tigers that live in different parts of the world look different. Scientists divide them into types according to where they are found. There is the Bengal or Indian, Siberian, Indo-Chinese, Malay, Sumatran and South China tiger. Three other types – the Balinese, Caspian and Javan – are sadly now **extinct**.

The Siberian tiger is the largest tiger of all. It runs through the snow on its big, padded paws.

Tiger culture

Tigers are important characters in some cultures. In China, the tiger represents strength and power. It is one of the 12 animals of the Chinese **zodiac**. The tiger is the national animal of India and Bangladesh. There are many statues and paintings of tigers around the world, and in some places there are tiger festivals.

Large eyes to see prey

Rounded head supports tiger's strong jaws

 Tigers are well known for their stripes, which can be brown, dark grey or black.

SIGN OF THE KING

The pattern of stripes on the forehead of a tiger can look like the Chinese character that means 'king'. 王

In China, the tiger is also thought to be lucky. These tigers decorate the wall of a Chinese temple.

Powerful hunters

A tiger's body is built for hunting. Its muscular body can run, leap and jump, while its teeth and claws grip and rip flesh apart. The stripes are important too, providing perfect **camouflage.**

Rippling muscles

Tigers are large – the largest weighing more than 350 kg – but they can move quickly over short distances, powered by their strong muscles. A fully-grown tiger can leap more than 8 metres or scale a 2-metre high tree or fence. Their shoulders and front legs are heavily muscled and are used to knock a **prey** animal to the ground, and then carry it away. The hook-shaped claws grip onto their prey to stop it from escaping.

 A tiger's back legs are longer than the front legs, which is ideal for running, jumping and pouncing.

Powerful shoulder muscles

Perfect camouflage

Tigers have more than 100 stripes which are useful for camouflage. The stripes break up the shape of the tiger's body, making it difficult for prey animals to spot them. When a tiger stands in the forest or lies down in long grass, it virtually disappears. This allows a tiger to creep up on its prey.

A tiger's orange fur with black stripes blends well amongst long grass.

The longest claw is about 12 cm long

UNIQUE MARKINGS

Tiger stripes vary in length, width and number and are like fingerprints — no two tigers have the same pattern. This helps scientists to identify individual animals.

Curved claws for gripping

Tigers pull their claws back into a protective sheath when not in use so they stay sharp.

Tiger territory

Less than 100 years ago, tigers roamed across much of Central, South and Southeast Asia as far west as Turkey. Now they are only found in parts of South and Southeast Asia, and in a few forested areas of Eastern Russia and China.

Jungle homes

Each of the different types of tiger lives in a particular **habitat**. The Bengal, Indo-Chinese, Malay and Sumatran tigers are found in **jungle**. Jungle, or rainforest, is a dense forest found in areas with a **tropical** climate. The temperatures are high all year round and there is lots of rain. They spend much of the day resting beside pools and streams and sometimes they stand in the water to keep cool. Not surprisingly, they are strong swimmers.

Unlike other cats, tigers like to be near water.

Chilly forests

The Siberian tiger lives to the north, in the mountainous regions of Northern China and Eastern Russia, where there are huge pine forests. This tiger has to cope with the extreme winter weather when temperatures fall way below freezing, the ground is covered in deep snow and the rivers are frozen.

CASPIAN TIGER

The Caspian tiger, which is now extinct, was found in Central Asia and as far west as Turkey. In the 20th century, the tiger was hunted and its forest home was cleared to grow cotton and rice.

The Siberian tiger has to survive the extreme cold of the Siberian winter.

The Bengal tiger

The Bengal, or Indian, tiger is probably the best known of all the tigers. It is the evil tiger, Shere Khan, featured in *The Jungle Book* by the author Rudyard Kipling.

Powerful hunter

The Bengal tiger is found in tropical jungle, in open forest and even in mangrove swamps along the coast. Small numbers are found in Nepal, Bhutan and Myanmar. As a top **predator** of the forest, it is not hunted by other animals. Being a powerful animal of about 3 metres in length from nose to tail and weighing up to 200 kg, it can kill large animals. It eats mostly wild deer but will also take wild pigs, birds and even the gaur, a type of buffalo.

The Bengal tiger is often found near rivers or shady pools.

White tigers

Rare white Bengal tigers have a white fur with pale stripes. There are several hundred of these white tigers living in zoos. They are mostly descendents of a white tiger called Mohan caught in India in 1951. White tigers tend to grow faster and become heavier than the normal orange Bengal tiger.

 White Bengal tigers have pale stripes on white fur and bright blue eyes.

Save the tiger

The Bengal tiger is under threat. Huge areas of its forest home have been cleared and many have been killed by **poachers**. A century ago there were 40,000 Bengal tigers roaming the Indian forests, but now there are thought to be fewer than 1,400.

During the 1970s, the Indian government set up Project Tiger, and created new tiger **reserves** across the country. **Conservation** organisations such as the WWF (World Wildlife Fund) worked to save the tiger, too. During the 1990s, numbers rose to more than 3,000 but unfortunately things started to go wrong. As poaching increased, tigers disappeared from some reserves. Poaching is difficult to control and is still a major threat to the Bengal tiger.

भारत
INDIA

25
1975
जिम कार्बेट शताब्दी
1875-1955
JIM CORBETT CENTENARY

The Bengal tiger is the national symbol of India and Bangladesh.

Tiger food

Tigers are **carnivores**, which means they have a meat diet. They hunt and eat other animals. Their sharp teeth and claws are shaped to slice through meat, and they use their powerful limbs to chase and trap prey.

Time for a feast

One of the favourite prey animals of the Bengal tiger is the chital deer, which weighs about 70 kg. Each year, a tiger needs to eat about 70 chital deer (or the equivalent weight in other animals). The tiger's habitat must have plenty of food to support it. If the tiger kills too many deer and they die out, it will lose an important source of food. Tigers prey on other creatures, too, such as monkeys, birds, badgers, bears, frogs and even insects. In fact, the tiger kills and eats almost any animal it can get its paws on. It will also eat rotting meat and fruit.

The chital deer is also called the spotted deer because of its white spots.

A powerful bite

There are 30 teeth in a tiger's mouth. The small incisors at the front are used for gripping and nibbling meat off bones. The four dagger-like **canines** (two at the top and two at the bottom) are used to grip and kill prey. The premolars and molars that lie behind the canines are large teeth that slice meat into chunks that the tiger can swallow.

 The upper canine is about 10 cm long, the size of a man's finger.

GIANT MEALS

A tiger may go for days without eating, so it gorges itself when it kills. A hungry tiger can eat almost one-fifth of its body weight in one meal – about 40 kg of meat.

Tigers usually eat the meat from their prey first, followed by organs such as the heart and liver.

Night hunters

It is dusk and a hungry tiger stands motionless amongst the long grass, virtually invisible. It is watching and waiting for something to move and is ready to pounce.

Silent attack

Tigers hunt mostly at night, dawn or dusk so they have to make good use of their excellent senses of sight, smell and hearing. They also learn where prey is likely to be found. They patrol areas, such as **waterholes** and rivers, visiting several times a night. Sometimes, they lie in wait beside tracks leading to a waterhole. When they are about 10–15 metres away, they charge forward. The tiger hits the prey animal with the full force of its large body, knocking it to the ground. It grips with its claws so the prey cannot escape. This sudden, silent attack is over in seconds.

When a tiger finds its prey, it creeps up slowly from behind.

Death bite

A small animal is killed by a single bite to the neck through the spinal cord, but a larger animal is **suffocated**. The tiger squeezes its throat for up to ten minutes until it is dead. Then, the tiger drags the dead animal under nearby bushes where it is out of sight. It eats as much as it can and then covers the rest. It returns over the next few days to finish its feast.

This tiger has caught a spotted deer fawn. Adult tigers hunt at least once a week.

SUCCESS RATE

The tiger is an expert hunter, but only one in every 20 hunts ends in a kill. In areas where prey is in short supply, even fewer hunts are successful. Sometimes the animal gets away, and the tiger is not quick enough to chase it. Or other animals, such as monkeys and birds, warn nearby creatures of a tiger's approach.

Living alone

Tigers are **solitary** animals that live alone for much of the time. They come into contact with other tigers to mate, and females live with their cubs for a while. The area in which they live and hunt is called a **territory**.

Territory rules

Once a female tiger has found her own suitable territory that has plenty of food, she keeps it for life. The size of a tiger's territory varies, depending on the type of habitat and the number of prey found within it. In a dense jungle with lots of deer, a territory may cover just 20 square kilometres. But in the vast forests of China and Russia where there are few prey animals, a territory may reach 450 square kilometres. The male tiger usually establishes a territory that overlaps those of several females, but is well away from other males.

Sometimes a male tiger is chased off its territory by a stronger male.

TREE HUGGERS

Tigers like to leave their scent in places where other tigers can smell it. Sometimes, a tiger wraps its front legs around a branch and gives it a big hug. Then they rub their chest on the bark to leave a smell. This is about the height of the nose of another tiger.

Tigers rub their bodies and faces on trees to leave hairs and scent behind.

Marking the boundaries

Tigers like to warn other tigers to stay away. They patrol the boundaries of their territory and mark boulders and trees with their urine. They use their claws to leave deep scratch marks on trees. Amazingly, this system works well and there are few boundary disputes. Sometimes the males fight over a female, but usually they stay away from each other. The tiger may be one of the best hunters in the world, but it is not a great fighter. Tigers avoid fights because they could injure themselves. An injured tiger cannot hunt and is at risk of dying from starvation.

The Siberian tiger

The tiger with the largest territory is the Siberian (or Amur) tiger of eastern Russia and northern China. These tigers live in the vast northern coniferous forests where prey animals are few and far between.

Keeping warm

The Siberian tiger is the largest of all. It has thick fur, with long hairs and a particularly thick ruff around its neck. This makes it look even bigger. Its cosy fur and layers of body fat help it to survive the extremely cold winters where temperatures plunge to -46 °C. The tiger has extra hairs between its paws for **insulation**. The Siberian tiger has fewer stripes than the Bengal tiger, and the stripes are brown rather than black. There is more white in the fur, too, which improves its camouflage against the snow. It is often confused with the white Bengal tiger.

The Siberian tiger has adapted to live in a cold climate.

Heat is trapped by 3,000 hairs in a single square cm of skin

On the decline

The number of Siberian tigers declined during the 1980s due to extensive **deforestation** and hunting. During the 1990s, the Siberian Tiger Project got underway. Scientists from Russia and the United States worked together to study tigers in their natural habitat. New tiger reserves were set up and numbers increased.

There are now estimated to be about 400 Siberian tigers in the wild and the same number in **captivity**. In Russia, forests have been protected or replanted to attract prey animals such as boar. Poaching bans have also helped to save tigers and their prey. But despite these huge conservation efforts, the Siberian tiger could become extinct in the wild within ten years.

This tiger has a much broader muzzle than the Bengal tiger.

About 50 per cent of tiger cubs die before they are a year old, often because their mothers have been shot.

Tiger talk

The roar of a tiger echoing through a forest is a sound that many animals dread. Tigers make other sounds, too, including groans, snarls and grunts. But unlike other cats, tigers cannot purr.

Getting attention

A tiger's roar tells other tigers to stay away. It is also a way of attracting a mate. When a tiger roars, its ears twist round so the white spot on the back of its ear can be seen. This may be a visual sign, telling another tiger that it is annoyed. Tigers do not roar very often, but when they want to impress a female they are very noisy indeed!

A tiger's roar only lasts for a few seconds, but it is a chilling sound.

Moans, growls and snarls

A mother tiger moans gently to her cubs, to call them. She makes other sounds including a chuff, a type of snorting sound. Tigers that know each other make a chuff sound when they greet each other. They also rub their faces to spread scent (left). An aggressive, attacking tiger growls a warning. It hisses or spits, and swishes its tail from side to side. A defensive tiger bears its teeth and holds its tail low, near to the ground.

LONG-DISTANCE RELATIONSHIPS

It is difficult to see far in a forest, so sound is a much better form of communication. A tiger's roar carries through the forest for more than 3 kilometres. This enables tigers to keep in contact over long distances.

This tiger is snarling with its ears flat against its head to say 'Stay away'.

21

Tiger cubs

A female tiger has her first cubs when she is about three or four years of age. The cubs stay with their mother for up to two years, when they are ready to live on their own. Then the female has another litter.

Helpless cubs

A female tiger is pregnant for 16 weeks and gives birth to between one and four cubs. The cubs are born blind and helpless and weigh just 1 kg. They have small teeth and feed on their mother's milk. After ten days, their eyes open. They are too small to wander around the forest, so the mother leaves them hidden in a den, such as a thicket of dense shrubs or in a small cave or crevice in the rocks. Sadly, only half the cubs will survive until their first birthday.

 The female hides her young cubs in a den so they are less likely to be found by predators such as snakes, leopards or jackals.

Hunting with mother

When they are about two months old, the cubs leave the den and follow their mother through the forest. When they are larger, they are allowed to go hunting with her, to learn the skills of catching prey. By the time the young tigers are 18 months old they are hunting on their own. Tigers stay with their mother until they are about two years old when they are chased away by their mother and find territory of their own. Female tigers stay in the same area as their mother but the males move much further away.

TIGER EYES

Everybody thinks tigers have beautiful amber-coloured eyes, but tiger cubs are born with bright blue eyes that gradually change colour to amber. This happens in other mammals, too. Some dogs are born with bright blue eyes that change within a few weeks to brown, and human babies are often born with blue eyes that change colour, too.

Play fighting is important because it teaches cubs how to hunt and fight.

Man-eating tigers

Tigers kill more people than either the lion or the leopard. During the 19th century, when there were many more tigers in Asia, it is thought that tigers killed hundreds of thousands of people. Today there are fewer tigers, and fewer attacks, but tigers are still feared.

Tiger attack

Tigers do not normally attack people, unless they are threatened or they are guarding their young. Sometimes the attack may be a case of mistaken identity. A person who is bending over, for example, may look like a deer. Fortunately, **man-eating** tigers are rare. Hunger forces some old or injured tigers to attack people, especially if they come into close contact with the tiger's territory.

Tigers usually attack from behind. These men are wearing masks to scare any tiger away.

Dangerous swamps

The tiger-attack capital of the world is the Sundarban swamps on the borders of India and Bangladesh. This huge area is home to about 600 Bengal tigers that kill up to 100 people every year. Scientists are unsure why there are so many attacks because the tigers are healthy and there is plenty of food. However, the people living near the swamps are very poor. Hunger forces them into the tiger's territory to find food. Sometimes, a hungry tiger leaves the swamp in search of goats and chickens in a village, and will attack people there, too, if the chance arises.

These men are trying to count tigers in the Sundarban swamps. They have a gun for protection.

Captured!

After a tiger attack, the local villagers usually go in search of the tiger to kill it. But because tigers are becoming rare, a man-eater may be caught and moved to a safer area, or taken to a zoo (below) where any injuries can be treated.

25

Tigers under threat

Tigers are at serious risk of becoming extinct. This **endangered** species has been losing its habitat and facing the threat of hunters. Although it is illegal to sell a tiger skin or use parts of a tiger's body to make a medicine, these trades continue, especially in countries such as China.

Protecting tigers

A tiger's habitat can be protected by establishing reserves and national parks. However, hunting (or poaching) is still a huge threat. Poaching has wiped out tigers in reserves such as the Sariska tiger reserve in India. Although there are anti-poaching patrols, it is difficult to protect such a large area.

 Tourists pay to see tigers in nature reserves, which can help to fund more conservation work.

Zoo animals

There are almost as many tigers living in zoos and wildlife parks as there are in the wild. Although it is better for tigers to be living wild, the zoos help to conserve rare tigers, such as the Sumatran and South China tiger. If numbers increase, it may be possible to release these tigers back into the wild. A small group of South China tigers, for example, are undergoing 're-wilding' training in South Africa where they are learning to hunt and fend for themselves, so they can be released back into the wild.

THE RAREST TIGER

There are fewer than 20 South China tigers left in the wild and just 60 in zoos. In 1960, there were more than 4,000 living in China, but the tiger was declared to be a pest by the government because it attacked farm animals. It was hunted until there were virtually none left.

Tiger skins and medicines made from tiger bones and organs can still be found in shops in China.

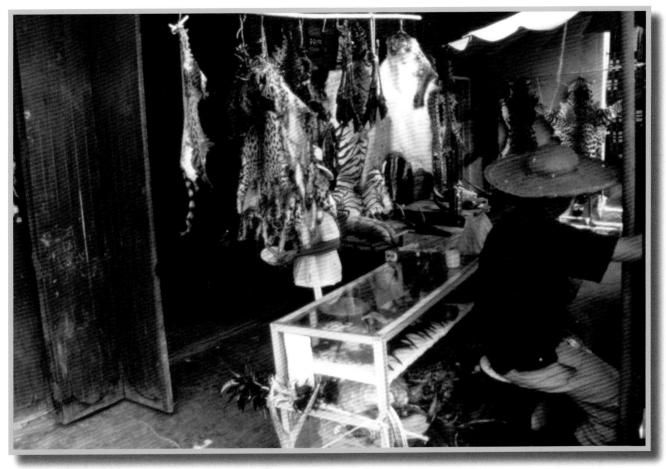

Facts and records

As top predators of the jungle, tigers are feared for their powerful paws, sharp claws and ferocious bite. They are amazing in many ways.

Largest and smallest

- The Siberian tiger is the largest of all the tigers. It is heavier and longer than a male lion, but not quite as tall.

- The Sumatran tiger is the smallest. The males weigh about 120 kg, That's similar to a female lion (lioness).

The Sumatran tiger is the smallest king of the cats.

Did you know?

- A captive tiger can live for 20 years, but a wild tiger lives for just 10 to 15 years.

- It is impossible to count how many tigers are left in the wild but experts estimate there are fewer than 6,000.

Tiger cubs

- A young tiger cub grows quickly, gaining up to 100 g in weight each day.

- Scientists think the white spots behind the ears of the tiger help cubs to follow their mother through the shady forest.

Names and numbers

- The Latin name for the tiger is *Panthera tigris*. The word '*Panthera*' comes from a Greek word meaning 'hunter' while '*tigris*' is an Old Persian word meaning 'fast' or 'arrow-like'.

- A group of tigers is called a streak.

- A tiger's paw prints are called pug marks. The pug mark of an adult tiger is about 15 cm long and 11 cm wide.

- A tiger can spend up to 18 hours sleeping.

Record-breakers

- The South China tiger has the fewest stripes, while the Sumatran tiger has the most.

- One of the best-known man-eaters was a female Bengal tiger called Champawat. She was believed to have killed more than 400 people during the 1930s before she was killed by a hunter.

Body facts

- Tigers have striped skin, not just striped fur.

- A tiger's tongue is covered with tiny, hard lumps that scrape meat off the bones of their prey.

- A tiger's saliva is an antiseptic. It is useful for cleaning their wounds.

- A tiger's night vision is six times better than a human's.

- A tiger's tail can be up to one-third of its body length. It helps the tiger to balance when running.

Glossary

camouflage
the colours and patterns on an animal's skin, fur or feathers that help it blend with its surroundings, so that it is hard to see

canine
a sharp, pointed tooth used for gripping and seizing prey

captivity
when an animal is kept in a zoo or wildlife park

carnivore
an animal that eats meat

coniferous
an evergreen tree that has needles and produces cones

conservation
the protection of natural habitats, plants and animals

deforestation
the cutting down of trees for wood to use, or to clear an area for building or agriculture

endangered
at risk of becoming extinct

extinct
no longer in existence, having died out

habitat
a particular place where plants and animals live, such as a tropical forest or desert

insulation
a material, such as fur or feathers, that traps heat

jungle
dense forest found in tropical parts of the world

mammal
an animal that feeds its young on milk, and has hair on its body

man-eater
a tiger that has taken to attacking and eating people

poacher
a person who hunts animals illegally

predator
an animal that hunts others for food

prey
an animal that is eaten for food by another

reserve
an area that is protected

solitary
living alone

species
a particular type of animal, such as a tiger

suffocate
prevent from breathing

territory
an area where an animal lives, hunts and breeds, and which it may defend against others of its kind

tropical
an area or climate that is warm and often wet, close to the Equator (the imaginary line around the Earth's middle)

waterhole
an area where water collects forming a large pond

zodiac
a type of calendar

Index

Web finder

Tiger Awareness
www.tigerawareness.co.uk
A charity supporting tiger conservation around the world.

Kids for Tigers
www.kidsfortigers.org
Find out about tigers and how you can help to save them.

Siberian Tiger Project
www.wcs.org/globalconservation/Asia/russia/siberiantigerproject
Find out about the Wildlife Conservation Society's work to save the Siberian Tiger.

Sumatran Tiger Trust
www.tigertrust.info/sumatran_tiger_home.asp
Find out how you can help to save the Sumatran Tiger.

Cyber Tiger
www.nationalgeographic.co.uk/tigers/maina.html
Imagine you're a zoo keeper. How would you look after the tigers in your care?